OUT OF THE ORDINARY

"This is a book about a bunch of people who don't know how to take no for an answer and who believe, sometimes against the odds, that the love poured into the most vulnerable young lives, echoes into eternity. Tim and the TLG team love to serve in obscurity, pointing to the awesome faithfulness of God and the glorious potential in each young person they meet. It's a powerful reminder that saying 'Lord, I am troubled by what I see, please use me to change things!' is the end of self-preservation and the beginning of adventures with Jesus who loves to rescue and restore. Read it if you dare. Then say yes!"

– Rachel Gardner, Founder of Romance Academy

"This beautiful little book is a must read for everybody who wants to learn more about big visions worked out through lives poured into the least, the last and the lost. Just the sort of stuff that the best God adventures are made of"

– Andy Hawthorne, Founder and CEO of The Message Trust

"An inspiring story of children's lives changed by local churches who want to genuinely serve their communities."

– Matt Bird, Founder of The Cinammon Network

"The story of TLG is inspiring. These are ordinary people who just refuse to believe that anyone should be written off. They have the faith to believe that God can turn anyone's life around and we are reminded in their story of the hope that sits at the heart of the Gospel. I am honoured to stand with TLG – their story is a shining example of how God can change lives."

– Malcolm Duncan, Lead Pastor
at Gold Hill Baptist Church

"Every day I see the difference the TLG story makes in broken lives. It is all true; inspiring, stretching and envisioning. Our cities need to see love like this."

– Simon Downham, Vicar / Senior Pastor
at St Paul's Hammersmith

"This is an exhilarating story. The vision of TLG is a nation changing one and I have no doubt that, together with God, Tim and his team will indeed change this nation. Enjoy the story and more importantly, join in writing the next chapter in their incredible history by helping them change 1000's of lives!"

– John Kirkby, Founder and International Director
of Christians Against Poverty

OUT OF THE
ORDINARY

The TLG Story by Tim Morfin

TLGBooks
Bradford
Copyright © Tim Morfin 2015

First published 2015.

Published by TLGBooks
National Support Centre, Hope Park, Bradford BD5 8HH

ISBN 978-0-9933317-0-1

Names of children and young people have been changed
to help protect identities.

Biblical quotations are taken from:

NIV - New International Version Copyright © 1980
by New York International Bible Society.

The Message (MSG) Copyright © 2002 by Eugene H. Peterson.

New Living Translation (NLT) Copyright © 1996, 2004, 2007, 2013
by Tyndale House Foundation.

International Standard Version (ISV) Copyright © 1995-2014
by ISV Foundation.

Printed and bound by CPI Group (UK) Ltd, Croydon, CR0 4YY
Book Design and Cover illustration: Gemma Parker

www.tlg.org.uk

CONTENTS

Acknowledgements   7

Foreword   9

Chapter 1:   The Heartbeat Begins   11

Chapter 2:   Lewis: Transformation   19
Against the Odds

Chapter 3:   Defining Moments   25

Chapter 4:   The Power of Education   39

Chapter 5:   Nowhere on Earth Like   51
the Local Church

Chapter 6:   This Need is Everywhere   59

Chapter 7:   Our Pile of Stones   71

Chapter 8:   Prevention is Better than Cure   79

Chapter 9:   A Unique Position   91

Chapter 10:   Momentum   99

Chapter 11:   Towards a Movement of Change   103

References   111

ACKNOWLEDGEMENTS

I want to say how grateful I am to the whole TLG team of staff and volunteers, past and present. It's such an honour to tell the story of what God is doing through you. Be encouraged!

Thank you to Louise Chenery for your tireless encouragement and skilful editing. We've done it! And thank you Gemma Parker for bringing your design skills to TLG at just the right time. A nice easy first project!

Thank you to those who pray and give generously to enable lives to be changed through TLG. Those of us who see the impact day after day are so grateful for the essential part you play in this story. Be blessed as you read more about what you are making possible.

I appreciate so much the trail blazing of the late Philip Haigh, who led a church out of its four walls to love and serve a community. And I continue to be so thankful to Pastor PV for his patience and willingness to let this youngster lead!

Mum & Dad - I'm so glad to be able to share in this book a glimpse of the way that your example in life and in faith has inspired and shaped me. Thank you for your friendship.

Rachel – it's my greatest joy to share life with you. Thank you for your partnership in the TLG story, and in our story together.

The bible, in the book of James chapter 1 v17, says: 'Whatever is good and perfect is a gift coming down to us from God our Father'. Thank you God for the gift of TLG and for the blessing of being able to be involved in what you are doing through your church.

FOREWORD

It has been said that 'mission is finding out what God is doing and joining in'. That pretty much sums up how and why I found myself beginning a journey of faith and hope in the inner city of Bradford.

A few years before I arrived in the city as a student, God was stirring up the congregation of a small church to reach out to the broken neighbourhood around. Initially under the leadership of Pastor Roy Lewis, the late Philip Haigh inspired a group of volunteers to open a coffee bar and to convert the former church manse into flats for the homeless.

From 1988, the church, led by Pastor Peter Vincent – PV to us – added a community cafe, a luncheon club for older folk, a parent and toddler group and a youth club. Run entirely by volunteers, this was ground-breaking stuff. That local church became a beacon of hope – a 'lighthouse' as it was called, in a community where there were few other bright spots.

This is the story of the birth and growth of TLG – The Education Charity, showing how God has used ordinary people in 'Transforming Lives for Good', to fulfil our mission of bringing hope and a future for children.

I am so grateful for the visionary call of Philip and others, who showed how a small, local church can make a big difference. Philip was always quick to say that this whole thing was God's idea, not his. It was the evidence that God was here that drew me in, fired me up, and gave me faith to believe that with God everything really is possible.

This book is the story of my personal journey of joining in with what God was doing in that church and in that community, of becoming gripped by the need and hopelessness of children and families, and being willing to do whatever I could to make a difference – and never imagining where that journey would lead. It's a story of God using ordinary people to do extraordinary things.

CHAPTER ONE

THE HEARTBEAT BEGINS

I was fifteen years old when I decided that the church's youth group, which was run by my parents, wasn't quite cutting it and needed me and my friends to do something to make it more interesting. So a typical teenager really! Maybe less typical was their response – letting me lead a group of other teenagers to plan and organise events for kids in the local area. I learnt so much! In myself I found vision coming from frustration – a strong sense of 'we must be able to do better than this'. As a fifteen year old, I was determined to see church become accessible for young people – to be speaking their language, meeting their needs, and therefore showing that there is a God who is speaking their language and able to meet their needs.

I had a middle class upbringing but for as long as I can remember our family had a heart to be involved in life that was more gritty and where needs were more obvious. My parents grew up in very working class settings. My dad was an only child. Tragically, his father was away fighting in WWII when he was born and was then killed in action two months later with the knowledge he was a dad, but never meeting his son. So Dad was brought up by my grandma as a single parent, living in a part of the city of Hull that was badly bomb-damaged. The post-war rebuilding plan was to move those families affected to a brand new "utopia" called Bransholme, which grew into a massive housing estate. Their church had been bombed, so as a teenager, my dad was involved in planting a new church for the new estate of Bransholme.

Bransholme wasn't utopia. As a child I remember walking around the housing estate. There was so much need - broken families, unemployment, and disillusionment amidst the recession of the early 80s. We would walk the streets, my dad and I, chatting to young people. We'd hear their stories and invite them to holiday clubs and events at the church. They were also running all kinds of community programmes, particularly traineeships for those who were unemployed. It struck me that for this group of people, worship was so much more than meetings on a Sunday. The role of church was well established for my mum and dad, – so having a heart for church and a heart for mission were just things that were really normal in our family life.

I was eighteen when I left Hull and went to university in Bradford to study Business. At that point, I really didn't expect that I would stay away. I was always quite comfortable with the idea of living at home and continuing to be so well looked after! I figured that fending for myself would have to come eventually, but why rush that? I was far enough away from home, yet not too far to take my washing back a couple of times a term! Growing up in a Christian family had so many benefits, although inevitably these are not always fully appreciated at the time. I'd had a great example and a really safe place to learn how to bring God into the ups and downs of life. However, I knew the first term of university was always going to be the make or break moment in terms of my personal faith.

It was around this time that the outlook for a small church in the community of Great Horton in Bradford was changing. Struck by the way the church was generally busy with its schedule of meetings while the community around was messed up, a group of volunteers, led by a man named Philip Haigh, launched a coffee bar, which later became a community cafe, known as 'The Lighthouse'. The cafe quickly became a social hub, running luncheon clubs for the elderly, and a parent and toddler group in one of the most deprived communities in the country.

Most significantly to the TLG story, among the densely populated back-to-back terraced houses of the neighbouring streets, you couldn't help but notice that large numbers of young people were without any kind of positive focus. Walking up or down the central Great Horton Road, or through the various side streets, always involved negotiating groups of kids just hanging out; Asian and white – although rarely together; young kids playing football on the street, older kids riding motorbikes, or hanging around a car. These children were growing up in a community with dealers driving through, where there were fights and neighbour disputes, and prostitution happened above the newsagent's across the road. Really aware of this huge need, I simply joined in with other volunteers from the church as we opened a youth club for these local kids.

By the end of my time as a student in June 1992, youth work with local young people was a significant part of God's call to me to stay in Bradford. It wasn't a 'flash of lightening' type of call, just a strong sense that I was being given an insight into the needs of a city that I couldn't ignore.

Just four years previously, the thought of staying after university would have been unthinkable. I have always been very close to my mum and dad. I have two younger sisters – Jayne and Rachel. Being the eldest and the only boy made for a really strong bond with my dad. We've always really enjoyed time together, conscious of the added significance of ours being the only father-son relationship my dad has ever had. I think his hope would have been for me to be involved in church leadership with him in some way. My primary school teacher did once say at a parents' evening that it was clear I thought my dad was God's right hand man! I don't know how I communicated that, but it was clear that's what I believed from a pretty early age!

Once I'd left for university, Dad never said, "You really should come back and do this." In fact, Mum and Dad talked about a time when they had promised God that they would support their kids in serving him wherever he called them.

That said, there was lots of encouragement to stay involved in church on Bransholme whenever I was back during my university years.

I don't know quite why or how it happened this way, but I was visiting Mum and Dad just before my final university exams - it was a weekday - my dad would often come home from work for lunch. I remember having a conversation over lunch telling them that I would be staying in Bradford. I remember then, as he was heading back to work, us standing by the back door, arms around each other, both of us crying. I guess it was the realisation of the enormity of the impact for them and, a bit of the grief for each of us that I would not be settling back home. I'm sure I won't fully understand what they felt until my sons are committing their futures to other places. Yet their heart for God and their love for me has always meant that I've been blessed with wholehearted support, prayers, encouragement and lots of good advice from Mum and Dad. However, that was a difficult summer all ways round. It was as if God was changing what I wanted to do with my life, and what I thought was important.

In the few years that followed I continued to play a part as one of a number of youth work volunteers. My faith was being stretched as I spent time with people who prayed long and expected God to answer, and got involved in a way that cost them time, money, energy and a fair amount of heartache. On Friday and Saturday evenings we were totally committed to engaging with some of the hardest-to-reach young people from the area. It was the heady days of PlayStation One, and courtesy of a donation from Sony, we had three of them, with TVs as deep as they were wide! There was no doubt we were aiming to change the world, or at least to change it for these kids. I remember the time we gave, the patience we showed, the long-suffering when kids kicked off, and our forgiveness amidst the annoyance when PlayStation games were stolen. Or worse, the moment one of the team could smell burning, only to realise that one of the young people had set fire to the hoody he was wearing! In our response, I know those young people saw something of the love and compassion of God.

I first rented and then bought one of the two-bed terraced houses just opposite the church in Bradford and lived first-hand with the needs of the community we were serving. On my street alone there was so much going on – families packed into two bedrooms with nowhere other than the street for their kids to play. There was often noise late at night from the takeaway at the end of the street, and my elderly neighbour would tell me of his fear of how much his community was changing. It seemed the residents of our small street had pretty much accepted the reports of prostitution and hard drugs in the second to last house on the right.

I couldn't help but notice that whilst the need was overwhelming, there was definitely a growing sense of connection between what happened 'in church', and what happened as we got stuck in to making a difference in our community. As someone who has been made by God to enjoy action, I began to see more and more that giving my Friday night to time with these kids was worship to God. When we came together to pray 'in church', there was a new sense of urgency as we asked God to intervene in the situations we were now seeing daily.

For as long as I can remember, I've felt strongly that the church needs to be relevant to young people. I have always believed passionately that Jesus should be accessible to young people, not just to Christian or middle class kids – but to everyone. I think about the teenagers who can't read the Bible or the words on the screen, or whose hyperactivity means they can't sit for ten minutes, let alone for the length of a church meeting.

The question was, what hope was there for this generation? And how do God's people respond if they find themselves in the middle of this kind of desolation? From such apparent hopelessness came the passion for disengaged children which has become the heartbeat of TLG.

CHAPTER TWO

LEWIS: TRANSFORMATION AGAINST THE ODDS

Lewis lived with his mum, two sisters and a brother, on the edge of the local estate. When asked where he came from, there were always puzzled looks, as Canterbury Estate Bradford was mistaken for Canterbury in Kent! I first met Lewis when he was twelve; he punched me. That was Lewis's way of introducing himself to most people! Periods of attendance at school were at best short lived. Exclusions, typically the result of fighting, resulted in months of missed education. Lewis hardly ever made it to the end of a school day and had no other routine in his life; yet every time we opened the youth club or had a church meeting, Lewis was there. That was probably the first time that this paradox struck me. It was apparent that he had found somewhere he could feel safe and secure where he knew he was loved and perhaps the one place in his life that would give him the right kind of attention.

It was the relationship built in that context which meant that Lewis would regularly ask for help. I would often be dropping him off at home and end up sitting in the car talking through ways to handle his anger towards his mum's boyfriend who often stayed over at the house. I'd listen whilst he shared stories of disagreements at school, which frequently ended in a fight.

Over the months and years, we as 'the church' became a significant influence in shaping the direction of Lewis's life, his instinct to land a punch gradually disappearing – with one notable exception. Lewis's regular involvement in church meant that even when there was a group of churches getting together to hear the Bishop of Bradford speak, Lewis would be there. On this one particular night we'd arrived a little bit late and found that the only spare seats were on the front row. Despite our prominent position, Lewis and the handful of kids from the youth club had made it through the meeting without any major disruption – a source of great relief to us youth leaders! As the final prayer ended, the Bishop stepped down from the platform and approached the group that had been so keen they'd been sitting on the front row! He obviously just wanted to 'connect' with the young people, but wasn't to know that when you approach Lewis you don't do it from behind and tap him on the shoulder. Well, in response, Lewis did what he had been doing for years: he swung round and landed an instinctive punch in the midriff of the Bishop of Bradford! There followed apologies all round, with Lewis assuring everyone that he didn't hit him as hard as he could have done. And the Bishop seemed to recover his composure, taking his 'connection' with the young people in good heart!

By the age of 15, Lewis had entirely stopped going to school and we realised we had to do something. Having got to know his mum well over the preceding few years, we worked together to present to the school an idea for Lewis to spend time on regular work experience with us. For an inner city school to be offered the chance to have one of their most challenging pupils off-site regularly, and engaged in anything remotely positive, was an opportunity they were not likely to refuse! For us, it was an opportunity to build on the relationship that had been established over the months and years, to give Lewis values and skills that would equip him for his future.

The deal was simple – Lewis could spend two days a week with us, if he went to school for the other three days. The initial focus was on practical tasks around the youth club building, with the aim of developing life skills and thinking about getting ready for work. But it was quickly obvious that, like any other 15 year old who had consistently missed school, help with Maths and English would be even more important. So he wrote letters on behalf of the youth club, with a thank you letter to Sony for the PlayStations, followed by letters with requests to video game companies, furniture suppliers and theme parks.

That investment in a relationship with Lewis – the one-to-one attention that he'd perhaps never really had amidst the chaos of growing up - really made the difference. Educational support was coming from father figures who were willing to show how much we believed in him, whilst challenging him to stick to the rules and commitments we'd agreed. We knew Lewis so well outside of his education, but rather than that familiarity hindering learning, we found it provided a consistency not available to him anywhere else. So much of what we were doing was about helping Lewis to learn how to learn - building the disciplines that would not only help a successful return to school, but also give him the best chance of making it in the world of work.

Perhaps against the odds, the result was a success. Lewis got stuck in and showed his determination to do well, with us and in his time at school. The school and his mum saw a real difference. The school then told us they had loads more kids like Lewis; how many more would we like? I was becoming increasingly aware of this massive need and I just couldn't ignore it. I knew I had to work out my part in what God was doing.

On and off over the years I have kept a prayer diary, making notes of the things I have prayed for and writing down those things I believe God is saying to me.

On the 4th October 1997 God spoke to me from the book of 1 Thessalonians 5 v 24:

"The one who calls you is faithful and he will do it."

My diary notes go on to say:

Calls not called. Present tense – not just a historical calling but a constant guiding and instruction.

I believe the 'calling' word can be overplayed. We are all called to live like Jesus and be good news. It is just living it and doing it. I don't think that there is anything super-special about the calling of those of us involved in this work. It seems to me that whatever we are asked to do by God, it is often born amidst frustration and desperation to see things change. God has put in me an ability to imagine things being different, and a concern for the church to do things differently. I saw that there are eternal things at stake, and that lives can be physically changed, hope brought and peace restored in this lifetime. I knew that week by week I had a growing sense that God had put me in this community, at this time, for his purpose.

CHAPTER THREE

DEFINING MOMENTS

We quickly began to reach out to many more young people like Lewis - struggling individuals who were not, for whatever reason, accessing school, but who would engage with us. The idea of not only providing fun stuff to do after school, but also a programme of education for these young people became our focus. It soon became clear that we needed to be a 'proper charity'! So TLG formally came into being on 31st December 1998 – a Christian charity meeting the social and educational needs of Bradford.

At the age of 27, I found myself leading the fledgling TLG team. Taking a faith-filled risk on young leaders is what was modelled to me, and what I've continued to do. This model worked because alongside me was the Church Pastor PV patiently mentoring, and the inspiration and encouragement of Philip Haigh – the pioneer who'd first got the church looking outwards and serving our community.

After university I'd taken a job with the pharmaceutical company GlaxoSmithKline – a great chance to do all sorts of business stuff - sales, project management, marketing, business planning and then a role in the management of learning and development. What for me had simply been about finding a decent job that meant I could live in Bradford, had quite clearly in God's way of doing things been one of the best leadership training programmes available! All that business stuff was exactly what TLG needed now. My heart had always been that I would not spend my working life in a big corporate organisation, but would be more directly involved in local church. Throughout my mid-twenties I'd successfully resisted invitations to become a Church Leader or Minister. Despite the confidence of those making the approach to me, I couldn't bring myself to inflict my 'visionary', 'strategic', 'systematic' leadership style upon a poor unsuspecting congregation! Yet as the TLG vision grew in my heart, I began to know that TLG was what God had planned for me.

So we stepped out, believing that God was calling us to make a difference for these kids. There was a massive gap between what we had and what we needed. We realised that to run an education programme from the church youth club we would need desks, chairs and computers, not to mention some employed staff to deliver the teaching. We would need a curriculum that these young people connected with around their interests, whilst at the same time helping them catch up on the Maths and English so many had missed.

The TLG story is built on God creating those opportunities for us to have faith in his provision. After all – first and foremost – this is his work and not ours; so our starting point has always been that God will provide. Our friend

Andy Hawthorne, founder and CEO of The Message Trust, writes about those moments when 'if God doesn't show up, we're stuffed!'. The TLG story continues to include so many of those moments, and in doing so, continues to demonstrate God's presence with his people. Each time God provides what we need, we see something more of his heart to reach children and families facing crisis in education.

In those early days, it was the sacrifice of those most closely involved that was the source of the provision. As a small group of volunteers from the church we knew the blessing of giving our time, with the hours spent staffing the youth club every weekend.

When it came to the launch of the charity, there was a whole new level of opportunity to give financially too. We just came to see that it is really good to give! As we give – time, money and encouragement – we get to share in what God is doing, and that is just the best thing. The Message translation of the Bible in Luke 6 v 38 says:

"Give away your life; you'll find life given back, but not merely given back – given back with bonus and blessing. Giving, not getting, is the way."

I have known that to be so true – life given back in all of its fullness. To get TLG off the ground there were some sacrificial amounts given from those that had some savings. None of us were earning really big money from our day jobs, but giving small amounts regularly made a big difference over time.

I remember when we first signed Direct Debit forms to be 'Hope Givers' to TLG. There were just a few of us giving what we could, and now we are among many, many people across the UK who give £5, £10, £20 or more each month so that TLG can help more children.

From the very early days I came to understand that the miracle of God's provision for this charity is not just in the money that's been given, although as you are about to read, that has been miraculous. There is also miraculous provision in the people he has brought. First of all to be a charity, you need trustees. So to Pastor PV, Philip Haigh and myself, was added an IT engineer Simon Bower, and Mike Royal – a significant name in the TLG journey. Mike and I had done some youth work together over the years – we put on a Christian music event called Club 17-30, which at the time we thought was so edgy!

I knew that Mike really got it in terms of the kind of kids TLG was reaching out to and the issues we were responding to. Of Jamaican heritage, Mike was born and raised in Croydon, South London, where he'd been leading church-based youth work, alongside developing his career in urban planning. From 1993 onwards, Mike and his wife Viviene were leading a church in the Yorkshire town of Keighley. One of the most enthusiastic people I know, Mike brought his big smile, big laugh, and big heart to this opportunity in Bradford. Initially a part of the trustee board, Mike joined the TLG staff team as National Director in 2005.

When it came to the people who would be with these kids day to day, there was a surprising twist. A couple of years after my arrival in Bradford, my sister Jayne followed in her older brother's footsteps. She studied Business in Bradford and, after graduating, spent a gap year with an Oasis Frontline team in Birmingham, involved in all sorts of church-based community work. On the basis of Jayne's taste of what was happening in Bradford, she decided to return to West Yorkshire and become the youth worker and fundraiser for TLG – our first employee! Jayne and I are quite similar in being able to look forward, develop ideas and focus on what needs to be done to make something happen. Her versatility and resolve to push through in faith, even when it's tough, have built a resilience into TLG which has been foundational.

The final pieces of the puzzle of how we were going to run TLG were coming together and there's absolutely no doubt we saw God working in the detail. When a friend passed me a name and a telephone number, with the strongest of strong recommendations for a lady called Helen Laws, I had to arrange a meeting. Helen is a unique person with a dramatic story of coming to faith in God and with a lot of life experience, most notably at that point with seven years supporting children in one of Bradford's most challenging schools. She was someone who undoubtedly had the ability to reach the most difficult children. Following our first meeting, Helen had a really strong sense that God was speaking to her about the opportunity of TLG – a clarity that would be crucial as the next few months unfolded.

We knew that we also needed to bring in someone who could fully invest relationally with the young people during the day. I started to think about who could work alongside Helen.

Dave Brons had been a university student a few years after me and was working in a call centre whilst he worked out what was next. Although he'd been involved at the fringes of things in terms of the youth work we were doing, deciding to take Dave on to work with Helen was one of those faith-filled risks that has characterised the way God has worked within TLG. The three of us now laugh loudly as we think back to the first time Helen and Dave met.

Helen was coming from the structure of mainstream school and Dave, the long haired rocker, was living life in a sort of post-student malaise! To add to the apparent mismatch, Dave at the time was regularly playing street hockey and a few days previously had taken a blow to his eye which was just getting to that nice purplish-black colour. We also now know he was suffering from post-viral fatigue. As a result, Dave grunted and groaned his way through the conversation. It was one of those meetings where I was just trusting that God was in this!

But God definitely was in this. Young people at crisis in their education during that school term had not only a loving mother figure in Helen, but also in Dave had someone more akin to a caring big brother.

Helen writes:
"My calling to TLG came totally out of the blue. A teacher friend that I taught with asked if she could see me. She told

me that God had told her very clearly that I was the person he wanted for a job at what was then a very small education charity. But I was happy in my role in a mainstream school. I didn't want to leave and so decided to ignore it, for a few weeks at least.

Having struggled with the idea at first, I decided God was in this and to be obedient to him. Before the start date, I met the young man that I would be working with - Dave. We were as different as chalk and cheese, but the Lord blended our skills perfectly as we learnt to work together. He also put love and admiration for each other in our hearts. We became the dream team!

The beginning of this journey wasn't easy for me. The first six weeks were heart-breaking. Every day I would walk up the stairs to the classroom, overcome with such a pain in my heart and I would weep. I thought in the beginning that it was grief for what I had left behind, but as the weeks went by Dave and I would often be praying for the kids and we were both crying. I realised that God had to break us for the work he had called us to do for him. We could never have done it without his preparation. It was as if he allowed us to share his pain for the children he was bringing into our classroom."

Before the term was out we had added Sam, an assistant teacher, to create a team of three supporting a group of up to ten young people each term. From the very earliest days, we'd meet and pray each morning before the young people arrived – now a foundation of our preparation for the day in every TLG Centre and the most obvious expression of our complete dependence upon God to change the lives of children.

For me personally, in the year before TLG formally began, as I was considering the direction of my life, another person had arrived in Bradford. It was one Sunday in September 1997. I was leading a church service and she walked in. I remember seeing her, what she was wearing and where she sat. As the service ended, with the church leader away that week, I was standing at the door shaking hands as people were leaving, so we got to shake hands and say 'hello'. She was called Rachel and had just arrived in Bradford as a student. Having finished her undergraduate degree she was in the city for a year to do her PGCE teacher training. Rachel doesn't remember anything about our first meeting! Not at all! With me being in a small church, 27 at the time and one of the leadership team, lots of people were looking out for a wife for me, which was a bit of a nightmare!

Rachel started to get involved in the church during that year and we became friends. She kept me at arm's length for a while, eventually agreeing to a meal out together, but dressing down in flat shoes and a brown blouse, so as not to make too much of an impression or lead me to think anything was going to happen! How wrong was she?

Rachel writes:

It was a simple plan. I would stay in Bradford for a year – long enough to gain my teaching qualification. Then when

I was finished, I would teach and inspire children to learn wherever God wanted me in the country.

There was a church just down the road from where I was living and so on my first Sunday in Bradford I went along. I don't really remember much about that first visit but I do remember I immediately felt at home. I became excited to be a part of a wonderful congregation with a forward-looking leadership, committed to bringing good news through action in the local community. So I settled into church life, getting involved in everything that I could, refuting any friends' suggestions of romantic suitors (one in particular!) as I was only going to be around for a year.

I had managed to keep most conversations with Tim within groups. Just before I went home for the Christmas holidays, Tim asked me if I'd like to go out on a date. I replied that I'd be happy to go out for something to eat together on the understanding that it would be 'just as friends'. I wasn't looking for a relationship and I wanted to finish the year without any heartache baggage. So I dressed down, didn't wear any make-up conveying the message in every way I could that we were resolutely in the 'friend zone'!

What I hadn't banked on was a fantastic night with the best company I'd ever experienced. Tim was thoughtful, generous, wise, and with a passion for Jesus that had 'feet'! With Tim, just talking about putting the world to rights wasn't good enough; he was somebody who had ideas and then worked towards implementing them. I left our time together inspired and with a little trepidation - he had the potential to mess

up my plans because I liked him and spending more time
together could challenge my 'just friends' philosophy."

After a great evening and many more that followed, we got
together. Beauty on the outside and beauty on the inside had
been my prayer to God when thinking about who I'd spend
my life with. From the first day we met, I was convinced of
the former! As we spent time I got to know the beautiful
person on the inside whose gentleness and heart for people
was so attractive. Rachel's passion for God and willingness
to surrender to him, inspired me. Our personalities are quite
different, yet we discovered such a unity, particularly in our
prayer times together. And being together was just great fun!
I managed to wait until December 1998 to 'pop the question',
and I married my soul mate in Bradford on 31st July 1999.
God is good!

The requests for TLG to help children were pouring in.
There was huge need, but we had such limited resources.
For TLG to succeed, I knew I needed to commit more, to
give more, to be more available. So I cut my employed days
at Glaxo to four days a week and volunteered that fifth day
for TLG. That felt like a defining moment – saying to such
a big company that there was something more important
than a career with them. Over the next two years, it seemed
that with so little, the odds were completely stacked against
the TLG vision; but we managed to make not very much go
a long way. With a handful of staff and a couple of gap year
volunteers, we needed a full-time employed leader, but we

knew there wasn't any money in the pot! In my prayer diary on the 7th August 2000 I had copied out from the book of Isaiah chapter 26 verse 7:

> *"The path of the righteous is level; Oh Upright One, you make the way of the righteous smooth. Yes, Lord, walking in the way of your laws, we wait for you; your name and renown are the desire of our hearts."*

My notes below this read:

Walking – We'll do everything we should do; Obedience, forward motion.
Waiting – for something more, that everyone would know it's the Lord who did it.

I remember walking in a park in Halifax with Rachel and talking about the need to be able to be focused on the TLG vision all day every day. She was amazing - not concerned about the finances, just concerned about the importance of doing what God was saying to do. We were expecting our first child, Ben, and there came this potential change on the horizon for TLG as things started to grow. We prayed a lot, week after week – together and separately - and had a real peace that I needed to leave my day job. This was the moment.

So on 25th May 2001 both Rachel and I left work on exactly the same day! For Rachel this was the start of what would be seven years at home after giving birth to Ben, to be followed just less than two years later by our twin boys Josh and Dan. For me, this was to be the beginning of being employed by TLG. I remember picking Rachel up from school, sitting in the car and saying, "Well, we've done it. Here we go!". We knew she wasn't going back and we knew that we had enough money to last us about 6 months. There was huge apprehension in leaving the security and scale of a big company. I guess it was a big decision, but not a difficult one. TLG had been put in my heart by God. We knew what was needed for this thing to progress and believed God would provide.

As the word got out to schools about the help we could give, requests just grew. All we had was the basic youth centre style classroom and the ground floor office we created in the house next to the church. There were six desks in the front room, I had the back room as my office and where the kitchen had been we created a reception! It was glorious!

I remember a meeting in November 2001 with a group of school teachers where we were asked if we could help out with a group of permanently excluded children who had been out of school for over a year. They loved what we provided, but for it to work they needed us to offer courses in music, business administration and sport. I remember being so confident – "yes, I'm sure we can do that", but all the time knowing that God was going to have to completely show up on this one! We would need to find the staff, but to run that in our current building was going to be impossible. Five days later a 'For Sale' board went up on the small warehouse across the road from TLG. We had absolutely no money, but was God going to provide in an amazing way?

In the Bible in Luke 10, Jesus sends out 72 disciples and encourages them to look for the person of 'peace' – not necessarily someone who shares their faith, but someone who will provide for them. Over the years, there have been so many people who have gone over and above what might have been expected, or even asked, in order to help TLG and the children we are serving. In the days that followed, the owner of that warehouse miraculously proved to be that person of peace. We didn't have anything more than a few thousand pounds. Even though we were praying daily, believing that God would make a way, it was still utterly amazing when God answered and the owner lent us the deposit to buy his building and waited 6 months whilst we secured the planning permission. How amazing is that? What a guy! What a God! What an answer!

CHAPTER FOUR

THE POWER
OF EDUCATION

The more young people we began to educate, the more we saw that even in the small community of Great Horton in Bradford, this was just the tip of the iceberg. As this book goes to print the most recent statistics show there are a staggering 307,468 exclusions from schools in the UK every year. Maybe the most shocking thing is that 43,707 of those are exclusions of children in primary school[1]. The number I simply can't get my head around and will not accept is that in England alone, an unbelievable 4620 exclusions are for children who are 6 years old or younger[2]. It's as if even before school has begun for these kids, they are being denied an education that meets their needs. They are being set on a road that leads to a loss of hope and any kind of future.

The symptoms are many and varied, including challenging behaviour and disruption. It's clear to us that family breakdown and dysfunction at home are the most common causes. I remember the young person who sat quietly in the classroom on his first day at TLG, not saying a word. During lunch, a staff member tried to engage him, asking what he did on his weekend. His reply was, "My dad died. I haven't told anyone. He was a dealer – the biggest on the estate. Now he's gone and I'm not safe."

Over the weeks that followed, the one-to-one opportunity of TLG gave the time for staff to begin to help him come to terms with his loss. We have worked with many young people who have experienced bereavement in the family – a mum, dad or sibling at a young age. Without the appropriate support around them, their overwhelming grief can rapidly transform into aggression and confusion.

Kim was one such young person. She was just a child when her dad died suddenly. The impact on her schooling hit hard:

"I had a really bad attitude in secondary school. I got so angry and would walk out of school. I began to like the attention I got from the class for being the clown and getting thrown out. I used to call myself thick all the time. If my writing wasn't neat, I'd screw up the paper and start again - I would get so stressed out.

But TLG helped me – I could tell them all my problems. They helped me catch up on the learning I missed and I finally believe in myself."

There are huge numbers of excluded children who have special educational needs, which in our experience can sometimes remain undiagnosed in mainstream school. For these pupils, classes of 30 often don't work. The Department for Education statistics show that pupils who do have a statement of special educational needs are seven times more likely to be permanently excluded[3]. We know teachers and school staff do a great job day after day to support the majority of children, but for the remainder the consequences of being denied access to education are potentially horrific. Statistics show that almost two thirds of the prison population have previously been excluded from school[4]. When it comes to male young offenders this is even higher, with 88% having previously been excluded[5]. For the 20% of young people a year leaving school unable to read and write to a reasonable standard, their chances of finding a job or accessing college are dramatically reduced. When the role models around are out of work, or in some cases involved in guns, gangs and various forms of crime, the link between educational failure and the criminal justice system is easy to see.

A far too common theme is that young people come to us expecting to die young. There was one lad I spent time with in South London whose dad and brother were in prison. One of his best friends had been killed in a gang incident and he was adamant that he wasn't going to live beyond his 18th birthday. It explains the high risk behaviour of disengaged young people – no sense that stealing a car is risky because there is nothing to lose.

A 2008 Department for Children, Schools and Families study showed the consequences for children struggling in school. It followed a group of teenagers not in education, employment or training at the age of 16, and found that one in six was dead within ten years[6].

There is no doubt in our minds that the need we've been called to is, in so many ways, a matter of life and death.

But how do we put back in a twelve-week term, what has been absent for twelve years or more? There's no quick fix and no single answer. We all need to know we are loved and that someone cares – that's a great start! Education is a way out of the cycle. It creates hope for the future. Parents and teachers know the importance of developing 'aspiration', but for our young people, it's often not about big dreams, but just believing their future can be better. When we help young people find hope, they have one of the keys to living life with purpose.

Few things can change the direction of a life in the way that education can. Of course that's universally understood in the developing world. When visiting Uganda with TLG young people in 2011, I saw the lengths that children and their parents would go to in order to access education - walking great distances daily and parents going without food and clothing in order that their kids could be educated. Their conviction was clear; the greater the education, the greater the life chances – being able to provide for their own families, find work that is fulfilling and play a full part in community.

As I came to understand the importance of education, I became excited by the opportunity to provide this in the context of strong relationships. Our starting point in developing TLG was that we would be both completely mainstream and completely missional – acting with professionalism to deliver the best possible educational support, whilst being a distinctly Christian charity that would be good news to those we are serving.

The format and approach we developed in the youth club building in Bradford between 2001 and 2005 has become the pattern for each of our TLG Education Centres. They are a unique blend of youth work and education, which do not look like school. That's important for a struggling young person attending a TLG interview for the first time. Tables to work at and PC terminals for everyone, in the mix with comfy sofas. Hospitality and the values of family are at the heart of what we do. So many children get themselves up in the morning, and come from homes where there isn't any food for breakfast. I know I can't concentrate when I'm hungry and I know from my own children how hungry growing kids get! So there is a coffee bar area in every TLG classroom where staff make tea and toast, and provide fruit or juice for each young person. We are caring for them by giving the very best start to the day.

The day is made up of six formal lessons, with slightly longer breaks in between than would be usual in a mainstream school. We use very small groups, allowing the personal help that's needed. English and Maths are so important if young people are going to be able to access the wider curriculum and move on. Then alongside IT and Science, we have always majored on the most active parts of the curriculum. Lessons in Art, Food Technology, Sport and Music are often keys to unlocking interest and engaging young people in learning. The centrepiece of every day is what has become known as 'family lunch' where staff and young people sit together and eat at a table. So often this is where insight comes, with great reflections, questions and surprisingly good manners!

Many of the small staff team in the early days of TLG had more experience in primary education and without doubt that influenced much of what has become the TLG way with teenagers. The "circle time" so familiar for 5 and 6 year olds as they sit on the carpet and talk about their experience and share their ideas, was the pattern for each work session beginning on the sofas with the teenagers. The depth of relationship that a primary school teacher creates with a child by teaching every subject all day every day, was key to gaining the all-important trust of damaged young people. When a child is left in the care of a family member so wrapped up in their own struggles against alcoholism or addiction that they are unable to provide for even the most basic needs, where can a trust relationship possibly grow? For so many young people, their really challenging circumstances mean that education is the very last thing on their mind.

When Callum was 14 his mum was sent to prison. Education was the last thing he wanted to think about as he struggled at home to cope with caring for his brothers. When Callum joined TLG he was 15 and couldn't read. Whilst at school, he had run out of his Maths exam, unable to read the questions.

Although he had missed out on so much education it was clear that deep down Callum really wanted to learn, declaring on his first day at TLG, "I'm happy because I am in school." Callum's transformation at TLG became evident as he grew in confidence, particularly with his reading and writing. During a music lesson, he went quiet and whispered to a staff member, asking them to sit with him as he recited a song he had written:

"This is how my life goes:

Fight, war, broken nose; go home to sleep; go home to bed; wake up in the morning – police by your side asking you to put on your clothes and come for a ride down to the station.

This is about my life in stages.

When I was a youth I was brought up in the back of a police station; court, fines, and probation. Kicked out of school – nowhere would take me. And I started to grow up, realised my life was messed up. I need to put my head down and learn a few stuff.

Now I've gone from a kid to a little man.
Now I'm grown up."

There was a remarkable change in Callum. He was speaking confidently in front of the group, developing his reading and writing and displaying a much calmer attitude. Callum's dream to study plumbing at college seemed doubtful when he missed his college interview. TLG staff attempted to arrange another appointment only to be told by a puzzled college office that

Callum had re-arranged the appointment himself and would be starting in September!

TLG supported Callum to go back into school full-time until college started. Callum believes he is a different person since joining TLG, and went back into school to re-take his GCSE Maths exam with confidence.

We have found ourselves with an incredible opportunity to help so many young people during the school day - those who are at the sharp end of social breakdown. And yet to close the doors at 3pm and say 'see you tomorrow' would be simply papering over the cracks. How much better to invest even more time in building the trust that gives the opportunity to really help young people change. Relational youth work is part of the DNA of TLG; evenings and weekends with young people is our history and from where everything began. This was the perfect opportunity for church volunteers to join in – to come alongside and encourage young people. Without doubt there are crucial conversations that happen in that setting that just wouldn't happen in the more formal class time.

The ultimate beyond-the-classroom experience with young people comes in the form of residentials – two or three nights away somewhere in the countryside. Our first residential was back in 2004, and they've become regular dates in our plan for every year since then. For so many of the young people we work with, it really is the case that they have never left their part of the country, and some have never even strayed far from their city. So outdoor activities with young people in the Derbyshire Dales or South Wales has been a great life learning experience. Increasingly we've themed a residential to make it an experience that really fits with the interests of the kids we have in the Centres. So our Music Residential enables young people, in some cases with little musical talent beforehand, to learn, play, and perform together. Our Heritage Residential took a group of young people on a traditional barge through Yorkshire – God's own country! And our Faith Residential gives young people the opportunity, in and amongst the usual outdoor activities, to explore faith and the questions of life. I once heard someone say that you get a year's worth of youth work done in one weekend away with young people. When our staff teams get back it probably feels like they've done a year's work! But the opportunity to go deeper in relationship, and to ensure the change in young people sticks, is invaluable.

I remember being so shocked when I met Jace, who'd missed 3 years of secondary school when he was referred to TLG. It's a story that takes a bit of coming to terms with, as his family had moved house as he finished primary school and his mum just didn't get round to registering him for a place at secondary school.

Jace writes

"It felt really bad not being in school. It was good at first because I had a few weeks off school, but after that, I'd just have to wait every day 'til my friends came back. It was just a lost feeling because I didn't know what I was doing with my life. It affected me really badly.

Before I joined TLG I was really bad. I was crying because I wasn't getting an education. I was scared and I felt like I was going nowhere.

TLG has helped me to bring out confidence in myself. Now when I go home it's a good feeling, and not a terrible one. I don't feel down any more. I have a feeling I'm definitely going to be doing something with my life – something I like, something I can make a living of and just be all round happier, knowing I'm going somewhere."

Once his situation came to light, the challenge was his returning to education. Not only closing the gap on what he'd missed academically but also entering the world of secondary school as a 14 year old, having spent three years outside education. The TLG team were able to help the family register him for secondary school and convince those involved that by the end of the TLG term, Jace would be ready for that huge step. A staff member went with him on the first day and then made weekly visits to encourage him through the ups and downs.

His growth in confidence at TLG, particularly through learning the bass guitar and then being part of the music residential, was a big part of enabling him to face those challenges of returning to school. I shudder to think of the alternative path: no education, no hope, and very few options for life. The story of Jace demonstrates powerfully how disaster can be averted and a life completely turned around. Success comes through great education that helps young people

Above Left: Tim's Dad (Mike) with Tim aged 13.

Above Right: Lewis when he first came to TLG.

Above: Jayne (centre) at the TLG youth club - just as we formally became a charity.

Left: Helen and Dave with their first group in 2001.

Above Left: Philip Haigh, who inspired us to believe that with God all things are possible.

Above Right: For Adam (right), who's cousin was stabbed that summer, the TLG music residential was a big turning point in his life.

Above Left: Hope Park before - the land that God miraculously provided for us.

Above Right: Hope Park Business Centre today - the home of TLG.

Above: TLG can make a huge difference in the lives of children, just like we've seen with Raven (left), Sophie (centre) and Danny (right).

Above: David Cameron visiting TLG in February 2007.

Below: Mark and Tim on the BBC Breakfast News sofa, September 2007.

Above Left: Luke's amazing progress at TLG celebrated with his coach and family.

Above Right: Tim & Mike with Ruby Wax - 'Best Charity to Work For' Award 2010.

Above: Building family and community at the first Family Adventure Weekend, March 2009.

Right: The Morfin family, (L-R) Josh, Dan, Rachel, Tim and Ben.

make rapid progress, particularly where they've fallen behind, but it's also about building relationships that go beyond the classroom and in so many cases way beyond their time on the TLG programme.

Over the years we increasingly saw that exclusion from school is a crisis for more than simply the pupil. We know that many of the parents of the children we work with will have had as many, if not more, problems at school, as their children. The result is a breakdown of trust with school, particularly where the pattern that builds up over months and years is one where whenever school are in touch, it's bad news. Combine that with the fear that surrounds any contact with social services, and the result is the absence of support to the families who need help the most. As TLG has developed, this has become one of the most significant opportunities for our partner churches. We seek to introduce a Family Support Volunteer at the initial pupil interview – someone who is available from the local church just to come alongside the family. It's wonderful that where that support is offered, almost half of the families will be keen to receive that help. Many times that's through visiting the family at home or calling to keep the family up to date with how the child is doing.

Church-based Family Support Volunteers are a listening ear, an encouragement and often there when the crisis hits – providing a food parcel, accompanying mum to a doctor's appointment, encouraging the family when they have had bad news, and on some occasions accompanying parents to court. In order to go deeper in relationship, our partner church in Bradford pioneered 'The Family Adventure Weekend' which has proved to be a really fruitful way to build relationship and support families to have fun time away together. Those of us who were part of the first of those weekends saw what a big deal it was for families who just never get to go away, to be out of the city together as a family with other families. Parents and kids doing outdoor activities together, making memories and building relationships.

So we are TLG - The Education Charity. That's our focus and our starting point. We definitely celebrate and work hard for improvements in Maths and English, whilst at the same time knowing that transformation is about so much more than just academic improvement. For us it's about the whole child - building a relationship that goes beyond the classroom, that touches families and makes transformation possible at every level.

CHAPTER FIVE

NOWHERE ON EARTH LIKE THE LOCAL CHURCH

When it comes to education, UK history shows that no-one has done more to bring education to the marginalised than the church. The result is a tremendous heritage of Christian faith schools throughout the country, popular with parents and pupils of all faiths and none. There are always those who would like faith to be a private thing, but the social reformers who are our role models – such as William Wilberforce, Martin Luther King and Elizabeth Fry - have shown what happens when God's heart of compassion is translated into action on behalf of those who have no hope and often have no voice.

In grasping the significance of the TLG vision, it's important to see this opportunity in the context of the way God has used the church to shape education through history. It's widely accepted that the Christian church was the first to provide mass education in the UK. In Scotland in 1561, John Knox and a small group of clergymen set out a national programme for reform, including plans for a school in every parish. The National Society for the Promotion of the

Education of the Poor was founded in 1811 by the Church of England. The founders were deeply concerned about the fate of the population, including children, working in the factories, mills and mines of the newly industrialised Britain. They set up the Society to raise money to build schools and pay teachers. These schools were to teach basic skills and also to provide for the moral and spiritual welfare of children. Their aim was to found a church school in every parish and by 1851, still 20 years before the state took any responsibility for education, there were 12,000 schools across England and Wales.

I find it really inspiring to read of the leadership of Joshua Watson[7]. He made his money in the City of London as a wine merchant and government contractor during the Napoleonic wars, then left business in 1814 at the age of forty-three, in order to devote all his time and energies to the development of church schools. The way he did that was by inspiring the local church to be at the forefront of providing education for those who were so poor they were excluded. Sounds like a very familiar vision! I'm so encouraged to see the example of those, who through history, have been willing to lay down other things and allow God to use who they are and what they have for him. Our lives are separated by 200 years but as I read about Joshua Watson, it seems we are men on the same mission.

When it comes to explaining TLG's commitment to local church, I will often quote Bill Hybels, Senior Pastor of Willow Creek Community Church, who says, "The local church is the hope of the world." We've seen that hope in all different shapes and sizes over the years. The support of the church was the backdrop to the change we saw in Lewis. The support of a church community was also very much a factor in the transformation of a young man called Steven. He was one of the very first young people that Helen and the team supported in Bradford back in 2001.

Steven's issues at school, as with the majority of young people TLG supports, were directly linked to the breakdown of the family. His home had an easy-going, hippy type approach to life, which made for an interesting clash with the boundaries of school. Excluded a number of times for fighting, Steven was referred to TLG. His moods were up and down. When he was good, he was such a positive force in the group. When he set his mind against something, he was a nightmare!

Steven says:

"I was permanently excluded from school for fighting. Out of school I was heavily involved in drugs. I used to go out and get ratted every night. I didn't want to go to school and I didn't want to achieve anything. I started off on cannabis and then ended up taking heroin. You reach a certain stage when you go out with your friends and they say "we're not taking cannabis anymore, we're going out taking pills". I was just easily led.

I tried my hardest not to get into TLG, but Helen, one of the teachers, tried her hardest to open the doors for me. She wanted me in. I came to TLG with such a big head and all I wanted to do was mess around and be rejected. But Helen didn't see that side of me. She just saw the transformation that could take place. I guess she had the vision that something was going to happen.

After a week at TLG my attitude started to change. I wanted to be there and attend everything. I was able to put my hand up and have the one-to-one help I needed. It wasn't just a quick 20 seconds, staff would actually sit down and explain it so that I understood it. Staff wouldn't leave me until I was actually confident in doing something. TLG had discipline. Some of the other places I'd been to, the kids took liberties because they could get away with it. At TLG we knew the boundaries and there was great motivation to work as the lessons were easy to follow and the staff were great.

I can't remember when I realised everyone was a Christian at TLG. When I got into the lessons I could see the difference in the teaching. The staff were student focused and wanted to give you 100%. They involved us in the after school stuff as well, inviting us to youth groups or to play football. It was fantastic for me because before TLG on an evening I would go out and take drugs, fight, mess around and get arrested. I had a choice of 'I can go out and take drugs' or 'I can play football and have fun and keep fit'. I made a good choice. Teen Challenge came to talk to our group about drugs and they opened my eyes to a lot of stuff. One of the guys shared his story about how drugs had nearly killed him and it hit me that it could happen to me.

I'm now a teaching support assistant with a lad who has special needs. I love the job and I can relate to the kids I work with. When they're kicked out of class or in trouble I'm there to go and help. It's all about second chances and giving young people a bit of extra attention.

If I hadn't come to TLG I'd probably be looking at a life sentence in prison or having the worms eating me. I've even become a Hope Giver now because I know where the money's going and that it will help other people who were in the same position I was. I've achieved so much since I've been at TLG and I thought I'd never achieve anything."

Steven would stay back and chat at 3pm, would find his way to the weekend youth club and to church on a Sunday. With his 'in yer face' confidence, he would chat to anyone and everyone. We witnessed the amazing way a young person from a disadvantaged family, found mother, father, granddad and grandma figures who showed love and treated him as one of their family. Watching the concern and encouragement Steven got from Dot and Ann, or Philip and Christine – his grandparents' generation – was increasingly a revelation to me of what really mattered. I'd spent a lot of energy in my 20s hoping to make the presentation of the Christian faith by the church more relevant, more contemporary, only to find that for young people like Steven, it was the time, interest, encouragement and love of the people that created the attraction. And young people so often simply look past any last century ways of communicating.

My conviction just continued to grow, that when it comes to making a long term difference, there is nowhere on earth like the local church. For me, the 'local church' in all its shapes and sizes is the thing that's most exciting, because that's where transformation comes together; the love and compassion of community, and the dynamic of God being at work. I'm constantly challenged by what it means for children and families to be recipients of that kind of love and compassion, but also to belong and provide that kind of support to others. My big dream is that education looks different in this country because of the difference that ordinary people who are part of a church are making. I just think of the almost one third of a million exclusions from school for children every year. I think of the likelihood that so many become one of the 66% of prisoners who were excluded. It is stunning to think that life will look so different for children and families because, through something that they thought was bad – a struggle at school, a difficulty in the family, an exclusion, God was able to work that for good in their lives. That's the thing that excites me.

As Steven was increasingly part of church, he joined the small group of church people meeting up in our house one night each week. For Rachel and I, Steven was someone who connected into our lives – he lived only a short walk from where we were living when we were first married. Life and faith are rarely plain sailing for any of us, and that was especially true given the chaos that continued at home for Steven. He'd phone sometimes or just appear at the door at other times when things had kicked off at home. I remember a couple of times taking him home when he'd had fights and fall-outs with his mum's boyfriend, and then going ahead of him into the house to negotiate his return.

So it was education, but it was so much more than education. We learnt what a difference just giving time can make - help and encouragement beyond the school day. Time and regularity; knowing we would be there night after night was a huge thing for those kids. And as we did this, a heart for something bigger than our city of Bradford was being stirred up in us.

CHAPTER SIX

THE NEED IS EVERYWHERE

In the summer of 2008, sixteen year old Connor Black was stabbed to death on the streets of Harpurhey in Manchester. After a row at a party that seemed to escalate, a young man in a hooded top was seen running away as Connor slumped on the grass. He was the second young man to be fatally stabbed that weekend.

There was a growing sense of urgency in our hearts as news reports flooded in of shootings, violence and stabbings amongst young people across our country. From 2004 we'd kept coming back to the question of whether or not this vision was only for Bradford. There was a time when I definitely felt yes – not that we didn't want to share TLG's work, just that we were so consumed by the need of our own city. The small TLG team talked and prayed together, and I think the best description of the change is that we had a growing sense of responsibility. We'd been given something that really had to be available to every young person and family who right now have burnt all their bridges in their education - children whose situation without TLG is hopeless. The possibility of local churches being there when the crisis hits, fired us up to do everything we could to push, to stretch, to work to take the vision further and faster. Life is so fragile, so temporal and we've got to make the difference we can as quick as we can.

I had a growing realisation of the implications of this bigger vision. I'd always seen my time at TLG as a long-term thing. As those early years unfolded I began to see just how long-term, and that I should be willing for this to be my lifetime's work. I began to talk to the leadership team about the commitment needed to really do justice to what God had called us to. I believe it changes the way leaders lead when they know they are going to be around to experience the impact of their decisions for years to come. In sharing my commitment with the wider team, I saw how God used that to inspire others to similarly be open to this being a lifetime and not just a season.

We'd had lots of visitors to Bradford over the years to see our Education Centre, but hadn't really seen anyone make a success of replicating our approach or the impact on children. I remember realising we would have to roll up our sleeves and commit big time to supporting churches across the country.

This was massive – way beyond us. It was nothing we'd thought about or planned for, and yet it was something that we began to realise was what God was calling us to do. We had so much to learn about how on earth we would grow from a local project to a national charity. Who could help us work out how to put TLG in the hands of local churches across the country?

I've always been interested in the way other people do things, so I took some time out to visit companies who were 'franchising' – sharing a proven model for local people to run. I wrote letters to the senior people at four different food retailers, expecting that I'd be lucky to get one face to face meeting. I did in fact get four positive responses! Amazing! I got to pick the brains of Managing Directors at Subway, Starbucks, McDonalds and Pizza Hut. As I drank their coffee and ate their pizza I got to see how, in a completely different world to ours, it was possible to have local ownership, with central support. This was great news – definitely our heart that TLG would be a ministry of a local church. It would be theirs and not ours, and with TLG support they would be able to do what would otherwise be impossible – to run a school! So all those lattes were worth it! But what about partnering with local churches?

We think Christians Against Poverty is such an inspiring organisation. They are a Christian charity helping those who face debt and poverty, and they do that through a network of local church based centres. John Kirkby (Founder & International Director) and I had met on holiday a few years before CAP began, and Matt Barlow (UK Chief Executive) and I were both youth work volunteers in Bradford when we were much younger! So we've walked the journey of charity leadership together – both organisations having their roots in the same part of inner city Bradford. The generosity of heart and sharing of sound advice from John and Matt were influential in this next chapter for TLG.

Convinced that those guys had much to teach us, I spent two days a week for three months on secondment at CAP. I learnt lots, helped support their management team in leadership development, and have stayed involved in their journey as a CAP trustee since 2006.

So from mid-2005 to Easter in 2007 we worked towards opening the first TLG Education Centre outside of Bradford. Crucial to making this step change possible, was the appointment of Mike Royal to the role of National Director. Having been part of our journey as a trustee and being an experienced church leader, Mike proved to be the ideal person to pioneer the replication of TLG with partners across the country. But the question we hadn't yet answered was: how big is this vision?

We'd drawn up a list of the ten biggest cities in the UK when first thinking and praying about developing TLG far and wide. At the time there were 66 cities in the UK... 'Why not?' I began to think! Whilst there would be some cities needing more than one TLG Education Centre and some towns also with massive need, this number showed the size of the mountain we were setting out to climb. For the small team sitting in a room in Bradford in April 2007 hearing me speak about every city in the country, there was every reason for some scepticism! We hadn't even done one at that point! Yet as ever with those God has put around me, there was a wholehearted stepping up to the challenge, with key members of the team beginning to think through the implications of developing TLG centres across the country. It was another of those defining moments. A step forward from which there would be no stepping back.

So the journey began. In April 2007, we opened a TLG Education Centre in Aston, Birmingham, in partnership with the Salvation Army. It was in this first step of developing the work nationally, that we began to see that our faith inspired others, with a marked increase in the number of people beginning to give regularly as Hope Givers – staff members who were sacrificially giving to the charity, our family and friends, and more and more people we'd never met who began to give ten or twenty pounds a month. It's that regular support – each person doing what they can – that enables TLG to keep growing new centres and to support children beyond the school day, making sure the change goes beyond the classroom.

Just as we had seen in Bradford, the first Birmingham programme was fully subscribed – with clearly no shortage of families in crisis and children on the verge of exclusion in Birmingham. The graduation ceremony at the end of that first term was amazing to be part of. About 35 people gathered in the TLG classroom that we'd created in part of the Salvation Army church hall – each student supported by a mum, dad or carer, and for some brothers or sisters, plus school teachers. The accents were different, but the stories pretty much identical to those of Lewis and Steven. And the faces of proud parents celebrating the first good news for their children for a long time were so special.

One of the first young people we worked with in Birmingham was Raven. She faced really challenging circumstances at home and played a big part in caring for her younger brothers and sisters.

Raven says:

"I ended up coming to TLG because I used to get in constant fights and I used to be rude to teachers. If I hadn't come to TLG, right now I think I would have been permanently excluded because I was on my last warning. Since coming to TLG I haven't had a fight and I've been more polite to teachers, probably because of the atmosphere at TLG. All of them in there – they're all my friends. I hope to achieve some goals and be the first person in my family to achieve some qualifications."

This was the church on the front foot – the Salvation Army working with TLG to bring hope to the last, the least and the lost. Awesome! But it felt so much like we were just at the beginning and the urgency I felt to do something in other cities was now even greater.

The launch of TLG in Birmingham came at a time when a number of young people had lost their lives through weapon-related violence in various cities in the UK. The gang culture, and 'postcoding' of young people based on which street they lived in, was in the headlines in a new way. For most of us postcodes mean nothing more than a bunch of letters and numbers we use on an envelope or a sat nav. But to young people in some cities, postcodes have literally become danger-zones, marking out no-go areas.

As a result, huge rivalries grow, as young people sense that crossing to the other side of the street could mean danger. As our profile grew, we were beginning to be approached by churches in different parts of the country, and it wasn't long before we were signing on the dotted line and partnering with a church in South London. This was followed by taking TLG to Harpurhey in Manchester- where incredibly we were given a unique opportunity to support a member of Connor Black's family. Adam was grieving for his tragic loss and was caught up in the gang recriminations that followed the stabbing. When he came to TLG he found comfort, safety and a lifeline, moving on successfully to college.

Mike Royal writes:

My journey with TLG began when I saw the need to look beyond my ministry which at the time was so focused within the four walls of the church. I felt a burden for the lost young people in my community who were disengaging with education and saw an opportunity to serve them. I'm so fired up about partnering with churches because I've seen first-hand the impact it has on their ministry. I see the difference it makes to families who are at their wits' end. We've witnessed the local church wrap its arms around some of the most vulnerable children and families in their neighbourhood.

I'm struck by churches like Yardley Wood Baptist in Birmingham. When they considered TLG they were small, doing very little social action, but they took a massive leap.

They said 'We are going to do this because there are needy young people in our community'. They had bags of faith in God and a trust that we were the right partner for them. As a result, lives are being transformed and the influence of the church has stretched far beyond their local area. People are drawn to a church that is seeking to make a difference with a gritty love ministry. It's wonderful!

At the time of writing, TLG Education Centres spread from Reading in the south, to Newcastle in the north and a host of cities and towns in between. We register a classroom in a church hall as a 'School' with Ofsted, and continue to see centres recognised as 'Good' when the inspection visit happens. The most recent Ofsted inspection of Bradford said:

"The School's provision is outstanding for social development. The School promotes a well organised and well structured environment, within which pupils are able to develop their personal and social skills by taking greater personal responsibility for their behaviour."

The result is that hundreds of young people each year are supported to engage again in education, returning to mainstream school. Whilst at TLG, 74% are making expected or better than expected academic progress, which is a really amazing outcome given the challenges these young people continue to face daily. Beyond TLG, 91% successfully return to school, or engage in training or work.

Successfully making that next step is so important given what we know is likely to happen in the lives of those who remain disengaged. We formally track each young person's journey for at least 18 months beyond the Education Programme, and we can see that 84% are still on course even a year and a half later. I will always look at those numbers and want to know that a hundred percent are succeeding, but in truth, given the road these kids were on when they were referred to TLG, these numbers are amazing.

Danny's story

"I had a rollercoaster of an upbringing. My mum tried her best to steer me in the right path but my dad disciplined me by giving me a good hiding. He saw himself in me; as a violent 'leader of the pack'. The anger that I built up against him I just used on everyone else.

In primary school I was excluded over and over again. I was always trying to be the 'boss man'. I had a lot of friends who would laugh at what I did and that would make me feel like an idol to them. In secondary school, I was excluded again and again. There was always a tiny part of me saying 'hold back' but I was too powerful and too well known to back out for fear of losing my reputation.

I was given a placement at TLG. I really looked up to the staff, especially Mark. He always looked out for me and I listened to him because I connected with him. Being at TLG made me think 'people here are going out of their way to do great things for you, why not treat them that way?'

I'm at Uni now, on a two-year fast track course of Business Management with Entrepreneurship and Property Management, so it's pretty intense but I've got big ambition. Afterwards I want to go into property development. I also want to do motivational talks for young people and I'm coming back to TLG to speak to the young people here.

I think my life is this way now because of God. There have been times when I've cried and said 'what's the point?'. Those times when I can't speak to anyone but God; he eases me. You know what I'm really glad about? That people like me now because of my character and not because they fear me."

For individual children and families, this success means that they get to see something of a God who loves them and cares enough to reach out through his church to help them in their situation.

Sammy's story:

"I look back to my first day at TLG - it was a make or break day and it changed my life. I was about to fail everything. No one would've accepted me back into their school - that's how bad my behaviour was. I had deeper problems. When I was younger I felt it was better to get drugged up and spend time with guys instead of sitting in a house I didn't feel wanted in.

TLG helped me realise that my decisions have consequences, helped me see a different side of life. I got good GCSEs and I plan to train, then start work as a primary school teacher as soon as my son starts school.

I love going to church, asking questions, learning how to deal with everyday problems. Everything's changed so much within the space of just a year and I'm so grateful."

CHAPTER SEVEN

OUR PILE OF STONES

Knowing that God is with us has been the thing that has made the difference. When things have been tough, when we've wondered where the money was going to come from, when reaching out has been exhausting, I want to know that this is God's thing. That he's got his hand upon it and will work things out.

When I read the Old Testament of the Bible, time and again God encourages the people to remember his goodness by building something. Typically it's a pile of stones, something they can see; and each time they do, remember what God has done for them. In 2008 we saw God work in such a miraculous way, and we built our own pile of stones! It was a demonstration of his hand upon TLG in such a massive way.

Thinking nationally had forced lots of issues for us, one of which was space in Bradford. Our Education Centre was based in buildings on both sides of a really busy main road, which had its risks! Our 'ground floor of a house' head office also had its limitations! Our passion is children, not buildings, but we knew that new facilities could be ground breaking in paving the way for our work in Bradford to be a flagship and, if we had space for office support staff, the replication could begin.

We had worked out that if we were to move to a new site, we would need about an acre of land. I remember speaking to one estate agent who simply told me that we had very little chance of getting what we were looking for. He told me, "I've got a client who has the money and has been looking for a site in and around Bradford for two years, and he's no nearer to finding it than when he first set out. You're looking for the same but you don't have any money!" But in one Friday afternoon phone call in the summer of 2005, I heard about a three acre site that was about to come to the market, in the best location imaginable. Then there was the catch – an asking price of £1.2m.

We've never had any spare cash – TLG is not reckless, but we do believe in stepping beyond what we can naturally provide, giving space for God to provide for us, and putting everything we have into helping children and families, rather than a savings account! It was an interesting trustee board meeting that September; all the tough questions were asked that are appropriate for such a big step. Ultimately it was agreed that we would do everything we could to find the money to buy the land. This was either complete foolishness, or an expression of our complete faith that God was in this.

At a lunch meeting in early October, Mike and I sat down with a representative of the owner and shook hands on a 'deal' for the three acres for £1.2m, with an understanding that we were going away to try and raise the funds. I remember walking back to the car knowing that we were asking for a complete miracle for TLG.

As a team we continued to pray- our faith stretched with the realisation of the opportunity and the size of what we were asking from God. It occupied both our prayers and our conversation.

I'll never forget the day that Rachel picked me up from work in the car and I spent the whole of the ten minute journey home talking about the land, how much money we needed and the probability of the deal collapsing if something dramatic didn't happen quickly. Her encouragement to trust God and to keep doing everything I could, was completely invaluable. Our three children were in the back of the car – our twin boys were just two but Ben our eldest was four. As we arrived home, I realised he'd been listening throughout this whole conversation. Without saying anything as we went into the house, he went up to his room and emptied his money box, bringing me £3.09 in small change, saying, "There you are Dad, the money you need to buy the land for TLG." As you can imagine, there was a part of me that wanted to say 'no' to him, to break the news that this wouldn't quite be enough, but I didn't. Ben's generosity in giving everything he had was completely the pattern of what God continually asks of us. Imagine his excitement, even at four years old, when I was then able to take him to the site and describe the vision of what TLG would be doing for children. And the impact on his faith as he saw an amazing miracle unfold!

What followed was a roller coaster ride like I've never quite experienced in leadership before. I wish I could say that my faith remained unmoved and that I slept soundly – it wasn't quite like that! I trusted God and yet found the limits of my faith and trust. I woke in the early hours of one Saturday morning, and will never forget the helplessness I felt. I walked the floor of our lounge, my bible open on the table, and for two hours I just called out to God in a way that I had rarely done before. I knew God was listening, and although I wouldn't yet be able to see any kind of breakthrough, as I read the words of Psalm 62 I was overwhelmed with peace:

> *"Find rest, O my soul, in God alone; my hope comes from him. He alone is my rock and my salvation; he is my fortress, I shall not be shaken. My salvation and my honour depend on God; he is my mighty rock, my refuge. Trust in him at all times, O people; pour out your hearts to him, for God is our refuge."*

I charted some of the twists and turns in an email to the TLG team on 31st January 2006 which read:

From: Tim.Morfin   **Date:** 31 January 2006 at 13:46
To: All.Staff   **Subject:** Answered Prayers!

Hi everyone,
Your prayers have been foundational throughout. As well as our morning prayers, a number of us met one morning in

November to pray specifically for the site. That morning we read Isaiah 42:

"I, the Lord, have called you in righteousness; I will take hold of your hand. I will keep you and will make you to be a covenant for the people and a light for the Gentiles, to open eyes that are blind, to free captives from prison and to release from the dungeon those who sit in darkness." Amen!

The owner Paul changed his plans. We worked towards a deal, only to find out just before Christmas that he'd had a very good alternative offer and sold the whole site to someone else. I've lost count of the times in the last 3 months I've heard Phil.4:

"Don't be anxious about anything but in everything, by prayer and petition, with thanksgiving, present your requests to God. And the peace of God, which transcends all understanding, will guard your hearts and minds in Christ Jesus"

It's just a couple of weeks since I got a reply to an email from Paul, the owner of the site, to indicate that he would be interested in talking to us again. Some very difficult circumstances in his personal life appear to have played a part in softening his heart towards TLG, with the conclusion being that he emailed me over the weekend to say:

"As you are well aware my outlook on matters has changed somewhat in the past few weeks. I now actually would like you to purchase the site and feel as though I had contributed in some way to an excellent organisation."

I said a few times in the past five months that if we get the site we want to be able to see that God did it... just like the man who lent us the deposit to buy his warehouse and waited 6 months for us to get things sorted. God has done it again for TLG! Praise the Lord! The site that was sold to someone else, came to us... at £570k, rather than the original £1.2m. Let's praise God! And let's tell the story of how God has blessed us.

Tim.

We set about giving thanks to God, visiting the site for the first time as a whole TLG team to pray at the end of January 2006. In buying the land we'd begun a journey towards one day having new facilities to educate children in Bradford, space for the staff team to grow and training space to support a network of centres nationally. We needed £600,000 to build a building and were talking in terms of that taking five years to fundraise. But timing is everything and what followed was miraculous timing.

Within just a week of completing on the purchase of the site, we heard of a Yorkshire funding programme that, although due to come to an end, had just been allocated some additional money. This meant there was suddenly £15m that had to be spent within 18 months on social projects in Yorkshire.

I arranged a meeting with the local council as quickly as I could! I thought it would be rude to ask for the whole amount, so I asked for a massive £150,000. They said, "If you can spend it within 18 months, you can probably have the money. And if you need any more, just ask!". Well it was everything that I hate about public funding, except when we're the recipients!

Not being backwards in coming forwards, it took me about a week to go back and ask for the full £600,000. "If you can spend it within 18 months, that should be fine" was the response! "Oh and if you need any more, just ask!" At that point I went back to the team and said, "I think we've got an even bigger opportunity here". What followed was a redesign of the building to make it about 50% bigger than was originally planned, particularly creating sub-let office space for tenants to share the building with us. With a full three weeks to spare before the end of the 18 month deadline, the TLG National Support Centre was completed and we received an amazing £1.6m grant.

Every aspect of the business plan came about above and beyond our dreams. By the end of the first year, the income from our office space, meeting rooms and sports hall, was fully paying not only the mortgage, but also the overheads on the entire building. When I give to charity I'm always really keen to know how much of what I give is going to the actual work. The blessing of this whole building thing is that with our core office costs now covered, every pound a donor gives TLG goes directly to growing support to children and young people.

My talk to the first TLG team meeting in the new building was based on Luke 12 v 48:

'For everyone to whom much is given, from him much will be required'.

If this is what God has given, he must have big intentions for the vision of TLG enabling the local church. Our opening celebration with more than 500 people was a great time of saying thank you to God. These facilities are now supporting the education of children and used daily to equip churches across the country to do the same. We continue to give thanks for this amazing blessing from God - a daily encouragement that God is with us and has a big plan for us to outwork.

PREVENTION IS BETTER THAN CURE

Is it possible to spot those who are struggling sooner? Would it have been possible to pick out Lewis in his first few years at school and recognise a child and family who would benefit from support? By the time young people are coming to TLG Education Centres, so much education has been missed and crucially, these children and families have often suffered years of struggle. The statistics are really shocking with over 43,000 exclusions each year from primary schools in the UK – that's serious trauma for families and damaging upheaval for children. For wider society and to a certain extent the church, it does seem so much of the focus of our intervention is when the crisis hits. I'm really struck by the words of Desmond Tutu: "We are pulling people out of the water who are drowning, when we should be going upstream and stopping them falling in."

We found these questions about intervening earlier were being talked about more and more amongst the TLG team. However that wasn't the only place where these things were being spoken about. Rachel's insight as a primary school teacher has been a major influence on me over the years. Having taught for three years before our boys came along, Rachel took seven years out of school to focus on, what she describes as, her class of three! She returned to teaching in 2008 when Josh and Dan started school. Perhaps being a parent and having the confidence that comes with experience, seemed to bring some of these issues into really sharp focus. "Why are we waiting for the problems to get worse before we do anything?" she'd say to me. In any situation where resources are scarce, that's inevitable, but when you see the bigger picture, things only tend to go one way. It is outrageous that as a society we don't do more, and do it sooner.

In those first couple of years back teaching, Rachel would tell me about children in her class with obvious additional needs that the system wasn't able to respond to 'yet'. Or children who, for example, had been doing well, but suddenly Mum and Dad were living in different houses, and there was a noticeable impact on behaviour in school. Then there are the children for whom the more formal approach as they moved through primary school wasn't giving them the outlet they needed – something that was especially true for boys. It does seem that there is often a temptation to expect that young boys can sit still!

The main thing we needed to know was, could a church be mobilised to connect with a local primary school and do something before difficulties got worse? So in January 2010, we asked Rachel to volunteer to lead a team exploring what would become known as TLG Early Intervention. As with so many things over the years, we were blessed with generous people giving their professional insight, blended with input from the TLG team. Unashamedly we made use of the insights of some very gifted people: several head teachers and deputy head teachers, an art therapist, a church children's worker, a specialist in child behaviour and a nurse involved in child protection.

Once we had done our extensive homework, there was nothing left but to have a go. Would an hour a week with a child make an impact? Would churches be able to find the right volunteers? What about the schools – would they be up for volunteers from the local church working with their struggling children and families?

Initially we began several pilot projects to test out the idea of church-based volunteers being trained to deliver a programme. The content of the one hour in school was about activities that fitted the curriculum, but also providing techniques that would help the child reflect on the emotional aspects of life. We knew that helping children identify triggers for their behaviour would be a crucial part of helping them change. What was obvious really quickly was that head teachers and schools were really grateful for this kind of help. In fact, just that year Ofsted had announced a focus for primary schools on links to the community. What better way to do that than to work more closely with your local church!

When discussing the recruitment of volunteers with churches, I was encouraged when one church leader said; "Over many years of asking for volunteers at church, this has been the easiest ask". Whilst tentatively moving to implement our idea, one of the big unanswered questions was about who would get involved. We hoped there would be mums with some free time, and retired folk with great experience. What we hadn't expected is that nearly half of the initial group of volunteers would be men. For primary education where on average 90% of the teachers are women, this was a dream! We had a broad range of people, from a postman starting early and available in the afternoon, to a self-employed accountant with some flexibility in his week, and one guy who was able to get his company to 'sponsor' his time and give him the hour each week to go into school at 9am to be involved in the programme.

The pilot centres quickly showed us what a huge demand there was and how even really simple strategies can have a huge impact. For John, the problem identified at the introductory meeting with his mum and volunteer coach Tony, was 'mornings' – he was a 10 year old who just didn't like getting up! The resulting agro at home meant lots of shouting and John eventually arriving at school 'on the wrong foot'. As a result of this he was often getting into trouble. Tony used the Early Intervention flow chart to help John explore each action and reaction to understand the pattern of what was happening. Tony helped John to imagine what it would be like if he did things differently. By making a change as simple as setting the alarm on his phone, John realised he could change the pattern at home. Through the weekly contact volunteer coaches have with home, Tony was able to directly encourage

John's mum to give him praise for any sign of steps in the right direction.

So dramatic was the change in John that everyone noticed! At home, John began to set his phone alarm and get out of bed and dressed without his mum having to shout. At school, the class teacher reported a much happier child arriving in the morning, and signs of more awareness of his actions. John reflected to Tony that as choices came through the day, in his mind he would literally picture the flow chart. Being in year six, the class had a short residential where John won the award for the best behaved pupil! This was particularly as a result of getting himself up and dressed and keeping his area tidy. The reward for that was to be able to attend a 'Golf Day' for gifted and talented children, with golf being John's favourite sport. What a great example of team work – church, school and home. This success gave the opportunity for the church to support John and his family well beyond the behaviour coaching. With John now enjoying secondary school, it's wonderful to think of the heartache this precious family has been saved. What might otherwise have been exclusion – unemployment – potentially even prison, is now learning, qualifications, and in the future a career.

It was clear to us from the pilot programme that an hour a week spent by a volunteer in school coaching a child had the potential to make a huge difference. In giving the go ahead to TLG's Early Intervention strategy, I knew that Rachel's involvement in overseeing the pilots might lead to her becoming more significantly part of the TLG team.

Having been in the TLG story, often behind the scenes, this felt like a major crossroads for our family. I remember sitting in Costa Coffee at the retail park in Bradford City Centre beginning to talk through the implications. What would the impact be on our family finances? What would it be like to work together? What about the missed opportunity of teaching a class of five and six year olds – the thing Rachel loves to do? The talking, praying and thinking continued for much of the spring of 2010, but ultimately the decision came down to our confidence that God was in this – not only for TLG, but for Rachel too. She joined the staff team in September 2010. The loss of a direct teaching relationship with children has taken some getting used to – she misses the classroom. Both being involved in the same work place does change the 'how was your day' conversation! But we have no doubts that, when our work is more than a job, when it's about faith and the whole of life, it's great to be involved together.

Rachel writes:

"For as long as I can remember I wanted to be a teacher. I think it may be that a part of me has never 'grown up' and I can identify with children and the way they think! My first class (when I was five) was a tub of buttons neatly arranged on the floor in front of me. By the age of seven my younger sister was my first live willing pupil who was bombarded with hand-written work books and activities. I helped in church kids crèche and then began leading small groups by the age of twelve. It wasn't until I began training for my PGCE in inner city

Bradford that I began to understand there were a growing number of children who were struggling with school at the beginning of their education journey, in reception class.

Over the next 14 years of teaching and nurturing my own growing brood of boys, my heart was drawn to those children on the fringes of education, who were struggling because of personal circumstances at home or in school. After many conversations with Tim and much prayer, we decided to see what a TLG intervention for primary schools could look like.

Whilst writing the Early Intervention materials and piloting the programme, my mission field was redefined. I'd been thinking too small: a class at a time and maybe eventually a whole school. I felt God say to me "But what about a nation? There are thousands of children struggling, thousands of children who with a little one to one attention, can have their futures transformed, thousands of children and families who can be shown love in action that would change their lives for good." Then he reminded me of the prayer I'd said in the early days of getting engaged to Tim:

'Lord, use our marriage to serve your purposes, that serving you would mean that we'd be more effective together than if we were apart'"

The initial focus of TLG Early Intervention was on eight to eleven year olds, but how do you respond when the head teacher says, "Actually, we have a six year old boy, Luke, who has already been excluded from one school and we've had to tell his mum that if nothing changes, we don't think we can keep him here." That was the terrible situation in another of our pilot centres that the coach James stepped into. So desperate was the situation that the school had coned off an area in the playground for Luke to play on his own. One of the 'My Time' exercises that Volunteer Coaches are able to do is to ask the child to draw around the fingers of one hand, and then think of the names of five people in their life who care for them and are able to help. Once completed by Luke, the Coach began to work his way through the names on the hand, beginning with Mum and thinking about how Mum cared and the ways she helped. The next name was James. "Who is James?" asked the coach, "tell me about how he helps." The reply was simple. "You're James and I know that you are here for me." I think that's incredible – the coach was the second person of five in this boy's life, and crucially a male role model.

The result of that help is that things really turned around for Luke and he remains engaged in school. And for his single-parent mum, things really changed too. She speaks of dreading going to pick up Luke from school, knowing that the class teacher would be waiting for her, to tell her what he'd done wrong today. What a tragedy. When I get the opportunity to pick our boys up from school, it's the highlight of my day. Such was the tenacity of James the coach in visiting the family and encouraging mum, she came to see how much the team from the local church were on her side. Mum began to link much more strongly to school, but also to link to the church. What we later came to find out was that Luke's grandma had been praying for Luke and his mum and that James volunteering an hour a week with Luke, and then reaching out to help the family, was an answer to prayers that had been prayed for years: that Luke's mum would come back to faith in God! And that's exactly what happened. What a difference an hour a week can make. Amazing!

Now being rolled out across the country, TLG Early Intervention Centres are proving really accessible for churches who within a few months of making the decision to partner with TLG, can have a team of fully trained coaches supporting children and their families. For some churches, Early Intervention is the next step in strengthening a partnership with school that's already based on assemblies and visits. For others, it's the first step in linking to the school. Queensbury Life Church was a brand new church seeking to connect quickly with the community and make an impact. They began with Early Intervention in one school, and on the back of their success there, are now in a second school with the third school in Queensbury wanting to come on board with the programme. For every church, it's an opportunity to link directly to children and families that are in need locally, and in many cases begin a support relationship that will continue beyond the coaching. There are so many examples of children joining in with the kid's activities of the church, and families accessing the wider support of the church. Whilst Early Intervention is proving really appropriate for inner city churches and schools, we're also seeing that even in what might be considered leafy suburbs, for example in both Tunbridge Wells and Harrogate - where we now have Early Intervention Centres, schools have children in need of this support. Families break down everywhere. Children have needs that aren't easily met as part of a class of 30 kids. So wherever there is a school and a church, there is the chance to be involved in changing the direction of a child's whole life, beginning with an hour a week invested well!

Little seven year old Sophie recently shared how coaching had helped her:

"Before I started coaching I was finding school tough because I had things going on out of school that were making me upset. I had my dad being a bit angry, and my mum and dad splitting up and a few of my animals and cats dying.

I felt school was a bit scary because I had some problems and I didn't know who to go to. I used to get into trouble for being distracted or annoyed, so I'd be taken out of class.

My coach was Louise. She was kind and caring and understanding. I think it's comforting that I know who I should go to if I get a bit upset or scared. The coach has helped me by having charts helping me to sort out what to do if I get angry. My mum, family and teachers have noticed how well I've been doing. As a result, I have been happier both at home and at school, and smiling a lot more.

Thank you for being really kind and sorting out my problems and helping me figure out ways to stop worrying. Thank you for helping me."

The stories of lives changed are so powerful, but so is the data of the impact made by TLG Early Intervention. After one hour a week of behaviour coaching for a year, over seventy percent of children are showing a significant improvement in their behaviour. For over sixty percent of the children coached, this is an improvement at school, with thirty percent of families also reporting a significant improvement at home. This aspect is a great tribute to the tenacity of our volunteer coaches who are coming alongside families and helping build a bridge between home and school.

The focus of Early Intervention is on behaviour, but what has also been striking is the academic impact. We have seen that improvement in behaviour is mirrored by academic improvement, and that a number of children are even making better than expected academic progress. Fantastic news - coaching that impacts school and home, behaviourally and academically!

These are exciting times for TLG Early Intervention. As I write we are working with York University on an external evaluation of the impact of Early Intervention, which will be a great opportunity to evidence the difference that the local church with TLG is making. We've recently developed Early Intervention to support the transition from primary school into secondary school, providing help at a time when children need it most. It's also been great during the past year to have Portuguese Christians join our UK training and take Early Intervention to Lisbon!

It was William Booth, the founder of the Salvation Army, who spoke about the social care of the church needing to provide both an 'ambulance' at the bottom of the cliff to care for the injured, and a 'fence' at the top. TLG Education Centres are the ambulance, but what's great is that with Early Intervention we now have a really solid fence that can catch children before the serious damage is done.

CHAPTER EIGHT

A UNIQUE POSITION

Being completely focused on helping children avoid educational exclusion has placed TLG in a unique position. We have increasingly become the place that the church turns to for partnership in supporting children facing challenges in their education. More and more we are invited to visit churches across the country. For those connected to education as parents, teachers, mentors, classroom assistants and school support staff, there is a huge opportunity to highlight the vital part they are playing in children's lives.

As we share stories of lives changed and the opportunity to make a difference, more and more churches are joining the TLG vision. We get to see churches of all flavours and all shapes and sizes, and know that each one is a unique expression of the kingdom of God and could have a unique ministry to children and families.

The TLG national vision has generated considerable interest in the media and amongst politicians grappling with the need for solutions to some of the biggest social challenges facing communities across the country. We have met with politicians from all the main political parties, making the case for getting in quickly and demonstrating the difference the church can make in local communities. Our first serious foray into this arena came through the Centre for Social Justice, set up by Former Conservative Party Leader Iain Duncan-Smith, with the aim of influencing policy across the parties. We were able to contribute significantly to the Centre for Social Justice Breakdown Britain report, with Mike Royal joining their working party on educational failure. This was the first time there had been serious interest from national politicians in what TLG do. It was great that our work was recognised. At the same time it meant opportunities for disadvantaged families to be heard and their needs seen.

In the summer of 2006 Iain Duncan-Smith challenged MPs to spend a week with a charity tackling frontline issues of poverty and social justice, and he asked if he could spend a week with us. He stayed with TLG staff, joined children in lessons and reflected with us on the opportunities to get a better deal for those failed by the system. When David Cameron visited Bradford in February 2007 accompanied by Michael Heseltine, he made a visit to TLG. It seems the usual format is that politicians come and they make the speech, but on this occasion I was asked to speak about the journey of TLG:

"...there are many aspects that set our work apart. The Christian faith that was so significant in the origins of that small group of volunteers, continues to be the engine that drives us. The approach we take with young people provides clear structure on the one hand, yet combines that with love and compassion.

We involve everyone, making the most of the fact that we are not 'school' or 'social services' and so we bring parents and carers together with social workers and teachers, all focused on the lives of young people being transformed..." [8]

This was followed by a discussion with children, parents and carers. Faye first came to TLG shy and withdrawn, as a result of the terrible time she had at school. She was so assured as she told David Cameron how TLG had made such a difference for her – giving her confidence and a huge sense of excitement about her future. Whatever we said or did that day seemed to make a big impression. In the end we lost count of the times David Cameron went on to use TLG as an example of the grassroots response he would like to see more of, in speeches, on BBC News, when interviewed on 'This Morning' and in numerous radio interviews. A few months after his visit he said:

"I have seen some extraordinary projects – places like TLG in Bradford – where tough kids are turned around through a mixture of discipline, kindness and hard work. They have shown that they are getting excellent results." [9]

Keen to avoid being politically aligned in any way, we pressed on to engage politicians from all sides. Several visits by Claire Short to our centre in Birmingham helped balance up the politics nicely! Claire took time to listen to young people, to really hear their stories, and came back to celebrate their achievements by attending the graduation and presenting certificates.

Since 2006, we've taken opportunities to influence politicians, and speak into local and central government where the opportunity arises. The issues of gang culture, youth unemployment and educational exclusion are never far from the news headlines. So there have been lots of opportunities in the news media to influence the way these issues are considered and highlight the good news of lives being changed. In early September 2007, we got an invitation to the sofa of BBC Breakfast News at Television Centre. Those best able to say it as it is are the young people we work with and so Mark came with me.

Just the journey to London for this sixteen year old from the north seemed to highlight the barriers young people can face. As BBC News wanted to film a short piece in what was then the recently opened TLG Birmingham, I travelled there the day before and then made my way to London. Mark travelled on his own from Bradford by train in the days when the BBC funded First Class travel! He was really uncomfortable, feeling out of place sitting in the First Class carriage. Then when he got to Kings Cross he queued for a cab, only to find that the taxi driver didn't want to take him to the hotel as he thought he wouldn't pay the fare. But it's so great the way these things work out. The BBC had booked a Hilton hotel, where I got one of the smallest single rooms, whilst Mark got a suite!

We were up bright and early at 5am to get to the studio. All very exciting, apart from having to wear make up! Mark's story is so powerful:

"When I came to TLG I'd been excluded from two schools and there were issues at home. I didn't really get along with my mum and things did not work out for the best. I ended up making friends with the sort of people that did bad things. I was being really silly in class, like the school clown. But also fighting a lot, throwing chairs around the classrooms and threatening teachers.

TLG really helped me in my education – I'd missed quite a bit of school. They built my confidence up to aim higher in a career. I wrote down in action plans what I want to do, where I want to be, where I see myself five years from now.

While I was still at TLG I learnt the bass guitar, passed grade 5 and applied for a course at the Leeds College of Music. I passed the audition pretty confidently. Now I am studying there on a foundation course which will lead on to a BTEC in music which I am hoping to get on in September.

That's basically it with TLG. They want you to be yourself and always have a dream in your life - giving you hope for every single day of your life."

And then I was able to explain a bit about how TLG works in providing very personal support:

"We've really sought to bring together everyone who has an interest in the education of the child. That's about bringing the family or carer into all of the decisions, together with school. Our work also involves the wider community through our partnerships with local churches who can support and help children and families through this difficult time."

It's amazing how many people are watching at 7.40am! Speaking live to millions of people about the opportunity to enable change in the lives of young people was undoubtedly a unique moment for TLG. Within a few hours we had many enquiries from schools and parents really keen to know if there was a TLG Education Centre near them, and churches keen to explore partnership. We also had people visiting our website and becoming Hope Givers in response to Mark's story.

With a national network of Centres and a growing profile, comes an opportunity to champion the cause of children and influence the system. Our DNA is grassroots, and so where there's a choice between time and effort lobbying government, or pushing on to launch another Centre for those in crisis, we'll always choose the latter. But there is no doubt that the kids we've been called to serve get such a raw deal from the system and we have to do everything we can to shape things for them. So it has been valuable to contribute directly to several of the Department for Education policy groups around behaviour, and support efforts to increase the quality of Alternative Education provision. When we have government ministers or senior civil servants coming to see what makes us different, and I take them, as I did recently, to the Parish Hall at Christ Church, Harpurhey, Manchester, they see something like nothing else in the world! A church putting faith into action, with a professionalism and excellence that causes professionals to come and ask the simple question – how do you do that? TLG has been raised up by God to equip and inspire the church, but if along the way we can shape the nation's approach to education for those who don't quite fit the system, that's such a great thing.

CHAPTER TEN

MOMENTUM

The need we've been called to is big – epidemic proportions when we think of hundreds of thousands of children in the UK missing out on an education. So when we think of the future, the TLG vision is a big vision. We do keep coming back to our mission – to bring Hope and a Future for Children. And each time we come to consider the scale and reach of the vision, it grows as we see ever greater impact and opportunity. We are no longer speaking of 66 Centres, but of 300 UK churches partnering with TLG to provide support through 300 Centres by the end of 2020. That is definitely beyond us! Beyond the capacity and the finance we have now for sure.

TLG remains as reliant on God's provision as we were in the very early days – that's a really sobering thought. But this is a God thing and I am utterly convinced his hand is upon it in ways I could never have imagined when I left the day job to make helping these children the focus of my life.

It's a big vision, but it won't always make a big splash. We're not doing what we are doing for a 'well done', although we all love encouragement! As far as TLG and our church partners are concerned, we're at our best when we're serving in obscurity – not especially noticed, but serving those who've had such a raw deal, and serving God by being involved in the stuff he cares about. So it's not about being noticed. But we do know that every time someone recognises and appreciates how lives are being changed, and the unique organisation that we are, the momentum behind what we are doing to bring change grows. It's like the snow ball that's already shifting, just got another big push down the hill! That happened in a major way towards the end of 2010.

There are two different national Charity Awards in the UK – one in the spring and one in the autumn. Being shortlisted for these big gala events is a huge thing, and so in the summer of 2010 we were particularly blown away to be shortlisted, for not one, but two awards. The first was in the category of Corporate Partnership of the Year, reflecting the opportunities we'd given to young people in London through our work with the law firm Osborne Clarke. The second was possibly one of the most hotly contested awards – The Best Charity to Work For. Given everything we'd set about creating, in making TLG a place where great work would be appreciated and potential fulfilled, being in the top six in the country was a great achievement.

When the awards evening came, Mike and I were right at the back – table 49 of 50. What an incredible surprise it then was when TLG was announced as winning both awards! What an honour to be receiving those awards on behalf of the children and the amazing people who serve them.

My appreciation first and foremost was for the blessing of God yet again upon TLG. A real sense that if there is anything good in what we are doing, in the journey we are on, then it's because of him. We don't do what we do for people to say 'well done', but when excellence is acknowledged, it's a great encouragement and endorsement that adds yet more momentum to the fulfilment of this vision.

Being a 'great charity to work for' remains really important to us. As a team, we love to have fun together; whether that's fancy dress, TLG Sports Day, or appreciating staff annually at our awards dinners. The day-to-day stories we come across and situations we are working with can often feel heavy. So we take every opportunity to laugh together, lighten that burden and appreciate one another. As Proverbs 15 v 3 says:

"A cheerful heart brings a smile to your face!"

From the very early days we've encouraged everyone in the team to take a lead whatever their role- we're not interested in hierarchy. We have a team culture where we are accountable to each other, yet free to use our individual gifts to make a difference. As a leadership team we make a point of personally helping to develop other leaders throughout the charity. I count it a huge privilege to contribute to our 'Fast Track' – our graduate salaried intern programme- which trains up leaders for both the classroom and beyond. This year we've added a second year for graduates to become fully qualified teachers, which is really exciting.

With new churches hearing about TLG all the time, and with us learning about how to grow Centres more quickly, we are seeing a step change in the rate of progress for TLG Centres across the country. And with Early Intervention producing such fruit in children helped to improve their behaviour and families supported, we have churches of all shapes and sizes thinking about how they could help a school and reach out to families in their community. I can't wait to see what will unfold!

CHAPTER ELEVEN

TOWARDS A MOVEMENT OF CHANGE

We are so privileged to be living in a time when the church is once again seeing the necessity of serving the poor in the way that Jesus did. It seems to me that the appetite amongst Christians to be involved in the needs of their community is huge. Martin Luther King Jr. told how,

---

"'The first question the priest and the Levite asked was: If I stop to help this man, what will happen to me?' But... the good Samaritan reversed the question: 'If I do not stop to help this man, what will happen to him?'"

When I see church communities thinking less of self-preservation, and taking faith-filled steps together to reach the poor and needy in their communities, it's so inspiring. It's great to be living in an era when church leaders are benefiting from the expertise of others, without feeling like they've got to develop everything themselves. The church I grew up in developed a community project training unemployed young people. They were aware of other churches doing similar good work, but those leading had to pretty much find their own way, make their own mistakes and learn their own lessons. If only there had been the possibility of adopting a proven model – saving time, money, and enabling a local church to be part of a national movement. The current popularity of such charities as Trussel Trust Foodbanks, Street Pastors and Christians Against Poverty now means that the principle of a social action franchise is well understood. Beyond those pioneers, there are many more proven models now being developed by organisations supporting churches to tackle homelessness, unemployment, addiction and more.

Even more significantly than the support available for churches to sustainably meet huge social need, is the change in the ethos and theology of many churches with regard to serving the poor. I grew up in the 80s – big hair and great music! It seems many churches of that era were outward facing and trying to be as accessible as possible, but as I look back I can't help thinking that the focus was much more on sharing faith than food. The church of today is realising again that Jesus said we should do both, and dramatically emphasised the point in Matthew 25 v 45 saying that:

"I'm telling the solemn truth: Whenever you failed to do one of these things to someone who was being overlooked or ignored, that was me - you failed to do it to me."

It really feels to us like TLG is the right thing at the right time for the church across the nation. Proven ways of helping children and families in one of the most significant needs of our time, focused on equipping churches who are increasingly seeking to serve the most disadvantaged in their community. Things are moving quickly. I am so excited to know that within just a few years there will be several hundred TLG Centres across the country, enabling thousands of children and families to be helped.

I have the privilege of meeting so many people who passionately understand the urgency of breaking the negative cycle. With each Early Intervention Volunteer Training Day, there is a growing movement of ordinary people playing their part - putting God's love into action to bring hope and a future to children. People like John, a retired firefighter, Pauline, a stay-at-home mum who has made time in the day, Katie, a childcare student needing more experience of working with children, and Jonathan, a graphic designer finding the time in his working day. Ordinary people who are doing what they can do.

I'm guessing if you are reading this book, you too may well be one of those people who understands the urgency of breaking the negative cycle, and breaking it as early as possible in the life of a child. I want to urge you to not just read about this story of lives changed, but become a part of it. My prayer is that through this book you will have been inspired by what God has done, and encouraged that he can do amazing things out of the ordinary. I trust you will be stronger in faith to serve where you are. And I really hope that you will feel inspired to join in with TLG in many different ways.

To see the fulfilment of the vision to bring a hope and a future to many more children, we will need thousands more prayer supporters and Hope Givers, together with hundreds more church partners and teams of Early Intervention Coaches. Would you become a Hope Giver and enable us to grow new Early Intervention Centres to change lives before tragic situations get worse? The average regular gift to TLG is £12 per month. Please give what you can afford. Will you also pray for us? We look forward to being in touch with you to share stories of lives changed, and update you on specific prayer needs and answers. It is really easy to support us online at www.tlg.org.uk. Thank you so much.

For those of you who are church leaders or have a passion to help your church reach out, our Church Partnership Forums happen monthly across the country. They are a great opportunity to understand partnership and to see how easy it is for a church partnering with TLG to make a lasting difference.

Children deserve a special place.

I find Nelson Mandela's perspective on social justice to be insightful. Speaking about the issues faced in South Africa, the former president said:

"Safety and security don't just happen, they are the result of collective consensus and public investment. We owe our children, the most vulnerable citizens in our society, a life free of violence and fear... and there can be no keener revelation of a society's soul than the way in which it treats its children."

Jesus went further, teaching that children are the priority, and the best representation of the kingdom of God. In Matthew 18 v 5 he says:

"whoever welcomes one such child in my name welcomes me."

He then told the parable of the lost sheep, about leaving the ninety nine to go in search of the one. Verse 14 says:

"In the same way, it is not the will of your Father in heaven that one of these little ones should be lost."

As for TLG, we are as committed as ever to stay both completely mainstream and completely missional – great education and distinctive faith. Our vision, centred on the local church and education, continues to grow. There are two very recent developments.

Realising that all parents struggle from time to time in supporting their kids through school, we've recently developed 'TLG School Kit'. It's a three session DVD - based course for parents of school-age children that shares principles and top tips on how to help children get the most from school. We're training up churches to be able to run the course in their church building or in partnership with a local school, which is a really easy thing to do. It's early stages but we are so excited to see how popular 'School Kit' is with churches and how support on this topic is really appreciated by parents.

Having taken young people in recent years from our Education Centres to both Uganda and Ghana to help in schools there, we've seen the exclusion caused by poverty in developing countries. Yet again it's historically been local churches who have been at the forefront of providing education. We're excited to now be exploring in Ghana how TLG can help a local church develop education for children who would otherwise be completely unable to access school.

After seventeen years of walking this TLG journey, I continually realise we've got so much to learn. I truly believe we are just at the beginning of what God will do. That's because this whole thing is about God's grace – him choosing to do something amazing and involve us in a way we could never expect or deserve. It is tough; at times heart breaking. But it is the greatest privilege to be involved in changing lives, and to be involved in something that God has so clearly got his hand upon. Before we had even begun to launch centres in other cities, I told the team that I knew this was what God had called me to do with my life. Being part of leading TLG is what I was born to do. Even if that were not to unfold as I hope it will in many more years of being involved in reaching these children and families, I know that it's not at all about me. God cares deeply for those struggling with life, and struggling in education, and I believe that care is being expressed uniquely through the local church with TLG. When we are at work in the things that are on God's heart, we can expect him to be at work through us. I think that makes for a very exciting future.

And what about Lewis – the first young person we helped and educated all those years ago? Where is he now? Well, he's now in his thirties, a TLG volunteer and he has become one of my best friends. He spends many an evening or weekend over at our house, and we see him as very much part of the family.

Looking back this year, Lewis's own words describe the change in his life:

"If I hadn't come to TLG I would probably be on drugs, in prison, or worst case scenario, dead.

I come from a one-parent family in Bradford. When I was eight we moved away to escape my dad. He wasn't a nice person. At home, my eldest sister got lots of praise for what she was doing in school, and my younger brother got a lot of attention because of his special needs. That's why I got kicked out of school - for attention. I'd wind people up, throw things at people and start fights.

I first came to TLG 19 years ago. Most people were standing around on the streets, drinking alcohol and just messing about, but I had somewhere to go. When I was at TLG I used to do computer work and I learnt all different things about real life. Afterwards, I went back to school, sat my exams and I passed. At TLG I was supported and loved by good people who helped me. I decided I wanted to grow up and work for everything I've got instead of messing about. I just thought 'I want to settle down and start living life'.

I now work in sales selling home improvements. I'm over the moon because I never thought I'd achieve what I have.

I have done voluntary work for TLG. I spent time chatting to the young people and telling them that it's better to walk away from their issues. I'd say 'if you get kicked out of school, you've got no qualifications and you have to live with that for the rest of your lives'. I told them I passed my exams and I'm enjoying life.

I got rid of the people in my life who were a bad influence on me. I see Tim most weekends and I can talk to him about anything – well, almost anything. What I can't say to Tim, I talk to Rachel about!

I've got qualifications that no-one thought I'd get. I love my job and own a car. But just being the person I am today, rather than the person I used to be, is my biggest achievement.

I've got faith and I know God's there. Certain things have happened in my life. It's made me sit down and think 'there's a plan, and I'll find out one day what that plan is'. I'm not perfect, but I know God loves me and I can rely on him."

The End, for now!

REFERENCES

[1] Exclusion Data from 2012-2013 Academic Year:
     England: gov.uk, Scotland: gov.scot, Wales: gov.wales,
     N.Ireland: deni.gov.uk

[2] Exclusion Data from 2012-2013 Academic Year:
     Exclusions for children 6 years and younger in
     England: gov.uk

[3] 'A Profile of Excluded Pupils' - DFE-RR190, 2012

[4] G. Berman & A. Dar, 29 July 2013,
     'Prison Population Statistics

[5] Transforming Youth Custody Ministry of Justice
     Consultation Paper, 2013

[6] Vaughan, R. (2009) 'Top Mandarin: 15% of
     Neets Die Within 10 years', TES, 7 August 2009.
     http://www.tes.co.uk/article.aspx?storycode=6019772

[7] Joshua Watson and The National Society. The Anniversary
     Lecture, delivered by Canon Charles Smyth, Fellow of
     Corpus Christi College, Cambridge, 12 October 1961

[8]   Extract from Tim Morfin's speech to David Cameron,
      February 2007

[9]   Extract from David Cameron's speech to the Policy
      Exchange, 31st July 2007